DROPSHIPPING

How to generate passive income using e-commerce advanced strategies, Shopify, Amazon FBA and eBay

Gary Loomer

The follow book is reproduced below with the goal of providing information that is as accurate and reliable as possible. Regardless, purchasing this book can be seen as consent to the fact that both the publisher and the author of this book are in no way experts on the topics discussed within and that any recommendations or suggestions that are made herein are for entertainment purposes only. Professionals should be consulted as needed prior to undertaking any of the action endorsed herein.

This declaration is deemed fair and valid by both the American Bar Association and the Committee of Publishers Association and is legally binding throughout the United States.

Furthermore, the transmission, duplication or reproduction of any of the following work including specific information will be considered an illegal act irrespective of if it is done electronically or in print. This extends to creating a secondary or tertiary copy of the work or a recorded copy and is only allowed with express written consent from the Publisher. All additional right reserved.

The information in the following pages is broadly considered to be a truthful and accurate account of facts and as such any inattention, use or misuse of the information in question by the reader will render any resulting actions solely under their

Your Free Gift

As a way of saying thank you for your purchase, I wanted to offer you a free bonus e-book called **10 Easy Ways To Make $2k A Month Passively**

Download the free ebook here: https://www.subscribepage.com/business2k

What is passive income and how can it help you to quit your day job. Imagine going to sleep at night, and knowing that your bank accounts are filling up.

In this free guide, you'll discover what passive income and 10 lucrative strategies to earn $2k a month and more.

Listen to this book for free

Do you want to be able to listen to this book whenever you want? Maybe whilst driving to work or running errands. It can be difficult nowadays to sit down and listen to a book. So I am really excited to let you know that this book is available in audio format. What's great is you can get this book for FREE as part of a 30-day audible trial. Thereafter if you don't want to stay an Audible member you can cancel, but keep the book.

Benefits of signing up to audible:

- After the trial, you get 1 free audiobook and 2 free audio originals each month
- Can roll over any unused credits
- Choose from over 425,000 + titles
- Listen anywhere with the Audible app and across multiple devices
- Keep your audiobooks forever, even if you cancel your membership

Click below to get started

Audible US - https://tinyurl.com/yxws2ssf

Audible UK - https://tinyurl.com/y3cudd4q

Audible FR - https://tinyurl.com/yyfmnuy9

Audible DE - https://tinyurl.com/y2sgmjb3

TABLE OF CONTENTS

INTRODUCTION

I want to congratulate you for downloading this book. We live in a time and age where online business opportunities and business models are proliferating, and it would be great for us to dip our fingers to try and tap into some of this wealth. This was one of the reasons why this book was written, to help you make money online using this simple method: Drop shipping.

All the chapters in this book will cover everything you need to know about dropshipping. In the first chapter, we will discuss what the whole dropshipping business model is and how it works. The second chapter will discuss how to start your very own dropshipping business by examining the top websites for dropshipping and the upfront investment on each website. We will then talk about the pros and cons of each website. The third chapter will explain how to find the most profitable niche so you can make the most profits and gain some of that wealth. The fourth chapter will talk about how to find the right supplier and how to build a great relationship with them. The fifth chapter will introduce a step by step process in order to find the most profitable product to sell which will make you the most profits. In the final chapter, we will discuss how to get targeted traffic using Facebook, Instagram and other methods so you can start to increase those sales.

I know there are plenty of books on this subject, and I would like to thank you for choosing this particular one. I know this book will offer you the knowledge you need to get started on dropshipping the right way.

Chapter 1: What is dropshipping?

Ok, so now on to the big burning question. What is dropshipping? Well simply put, dropshipping is a business model where you are going to act as the "middle man." So mainly what you are going to do is find a product from a supplier at a really low price. And thereafter for this product, you make an online store or sell on an online store. One way or another you will need a storefront from where you can display your products, sell and collect payments. On this storefront, you would upload compelling product photos and description.

On your store or website, you will sell the product at a much higher price than the price you will be paying for it. You then target your store to specific groups of people who will be interested in purchasing your product. Once they buy the product from you, you will then go to your supplier and buy it, and directly ship it to the buyer without you even touching the product. This leaves you with the profit in your pocket.

Now that you have a basic introduction to what dropshipping is, let me talk to you about the benefits of dropshipping compared to other business models. There are a lot of benefits to doing a dropshipping style of business. The main one is that you will not be holding any kind of inventory. This means you won't have to make any big upfront investments in buying a whole lot of products or renting out a warehouse where you have to store it. Another great benefit with this style of business model is that you will not have to worry about shipping the product. The supplier will take care of that for you. Sometimes depending on where you shop the product from, the supplier may even take care of the customer services side of things. This may also include refunds, late delivery etc.

Ths may feel like a surprise for some of us, as we have this notion that to set up an import/export business or retail business you need to have significant upfront investments and a big storage place where you can keep all your products. Well, I am here to tell you that those days are long gone. The truth is that you don't need a whole lot of upfront investment to start your very own business, all you need is a laptop or a computer, a high-quality product which you can get for cheap, a storefront and an audience. No large upfront investment, no warehouse to rent, nothing! This is why dropshipping is one of the best business models and has so much potential to give back great rewards.

There are two ways you can go about starting your dropshipping business which we will cover in-depth within this chapter. The first way is online dropshipping. This is your typical way of dropshipping which is done by most people when they first start their dropshipping business. The second one is warehouse dropshipping. Although it requires a little more upfront investment, it still has a lot of benefits to it. Let's dive deep into these two dropshipping methods.

Online dropshipping

Online dropshipping is one the most common ways people decide to start up their dropshipping business these days. This is the method which comes to mind when people talk about dropshipping. In this method you will have to find a supplier who can provide you with high-quality products for a cheap price. One thing you have to make sure when finding your supplier is that they will have the ability to deliver the product for you directly to the buyer without you having to being involved (Otherwise the customer management headache you will have to face, may not be worth using this method). Using this method, you will most likely have to make your own website like using Shopify to make your online store, or if you don't want to create your website you can use sites like eBay, Amazon marketplace, etc. We will discuss later in this book which websites to choose for your dropshipping business.

Now, if you decide to use this method for your dropshipping you will have to make sure that you have a safe and secure way of collecting payments from your client. Not only will it help you get paid safely, but it will also make your costumers feel safe once they decide to make a purchase on your website or product. If you are thinking about creating your own e-commerce website for your products, then make sure you add a trust badge on your website to help customers feel safe whilst using your site. Ensure you do research into a secure payment gateway to apply for your website. If you're using Shopify as your website, you will not need to worry about trust as the website already has security on the site. Another great tip is to have a PayPal account, as many people use PayPal to make purchases on your website. So if you want to get paid, make a PayPal account.

Now, I want to discuss the benefits of using online dropshipping for your business. Like I mentioned before, you don't have to hold any inventory, meaning there's no need to buy any products in bulk or rent out a warehouse where you can store your products. All you are simply going to do is make a website, upload the product on your website with a markup and once someone purchases the product you will simply give the shipping information to your supplier and he or she will mail it out to them! Plain and simple. The only thing you might need an investment in would be buying a domain name for your website, which I highly recommend. Domain costs are reasonable and would probably cost you around $10 a year. Also if you are not a programmer or can't code, then you may have to use a website platform to start selling your products and to collect payments, which will cost you additionally $30 to $120 a month (depending on which website platform you decide to use). If you want, you can pay for the whole year in one go with your website provider, which will save you money.

Just like any business model, there can be some challenges to this method so it would be a good idea to address them. The main one is shipping times. We live in a world where some companies ship products within a day or ordering. Most of the time the supplier you will be working with will be from China, so the orders for your clients will be shipped out of China. For you to actually make a profit on your sale you will have to use the most cost efficient way of shipping, which will result in slower shipping times. Now this isn't a total deal breaker, but people are impatient, some more than others. So if you don't pick the right supplier and shipping methods, you can expect to get cancellations as people will not be happy with the delays in delivery. Not all your orders will get refunded, but some may. It's unrealistic to expect shipping times of one day like some of your competitors offer as they are large cooperatives with an established infrastructure. However, I will give some tips and techniques to get faster delivery to your client using dropshipping, later in the book.

Another drawback with this business model is that you won't be able to determine the quality of the products which you're going to be selling, not unless you buy them for yourself first, which I would recommend you do before putting them into your store. This will lower the risk of your products getting refunded for quality issues. One more thing you need to consider is driving traffic to your product. Since you won't be affiliated with any big companies, you will have to drive traffic to your own website or storefront using paid advertisements.

Warehouse dropshipping

In this method, you will have to buy a certain quantity of products upfront. And as you have these products with you, you have the benefit of faster shipping, which will allow you to have fewer chances of cancellations and have better customer satisfaction, which is different from the online dropshipping method.

So, let's dwell on how warehouse dropshipping exactly works. The first thing to remember is that you will be selling your product on a website like Amazon. You can still use the warehouse dropshipping method with your own website but you will have to rent out a warehouse, and shipping would be your responsibility. Companies like Amazon will let you store products in their warehouse and ship the products out for you, which is why it is recommended to work with a big company when doing a warehouse dropshipping model. You find a product for cheap or buy it from a warehouse in bulk, then you will ship your inventory to the company's warehouse. Once that is done you can sit back and see the profits in your bank account; you don't have to worry about anything like customer service, making a website, or capturing a payment-- nothing! The company will take care of everything for you.

But, the upfront investment to start this business model is higher than online dropshipping. Let me break it down for you. Depending on the product and how much of it you buy, you are looking to spend $1,000 to $2,000 on your inventory. Companies also charge you to have a seller's account. That could start from around $39.99 and go up depending on how many products you sell, plus a fee for every product shipped. So as you can see, there is quite a bit more upfront investment compared to the online dropshipping method. Although this method has a big upfront investment it also has some positives to consider.

There are a lot of benefits with this dropshipping method, so let us talk about them. The best benefit by using this dropshipping method is that you can actually quality check the products before you decide to sell them. It is important that you check your product quality before you ship them off in order for your refund rates to be low. Another great benefit with warehouse dropshipping is that, once you have shipped it to the company warehouse, you don't have to worry about anything else. The company will take care of the shipping, etc. Another huge benefit with this business model is that you will not have to worry about advertising your product as much as the online dropshipping method. Since your product will be listed in the company website, which already gets a lot of traffic, you won't have to worry about promoting your product too much, which could mean less paid advertisement and more money in your pocket.

All that being said, there is one major flaw with this method of dropshipping. There is no guarantee all your products will sell, if any. Even though you will be listing your product on a website which gets a lot of traffic, it won't always equate to sales. Remember there will be a lot of products you will be competing with on the website, so making sure your product sells is crucial if you don't want to lose your investment.

So hopefully, you now know what dropshipping is and the different ways you can go about starting your dropshipping business. If you are still confused, then don't worry. Keep reading, and it will start to get less confusing as we go along in this book, and hopefully, everyone reading this book now has an understanding on what it takes to start a dropshipping business. In my opinion, dropshipping is one of the most straightforward business models to scale up and make money on, so keep on reading.

CHAPTER 2: HOW TO START A DROPSHIPPING BUSINESS

Now, since you now have an idea on the types of dropshipping business models and a rough idea on how to go about starting your own dropshipping business, I would really like to get into the specifics of starting your very own dropshipping business. Now, if you have been doing some research online on dropshipping, you might have heard of a lot of websites where you can start your dropshipping business, but for this chapter, we will stick with the top three websites. Those three would be Shopify, Amazon,and eBay.

The reason why we will be only going through these three websites is that every other dropshipping platform is mimicking these three websites, so there's no need to worry about learning each dropshipping website, as they are similar to the top three. We will go into details on each of the websites, we will discuss things such as the exact startup cost of each website, how to get paid on each website and how much legwork it will take to get started on each website. One more thing I would really like to talk about is the potential income with each website, as there are a lot of misconceptions floating around the internet regarding this topic, so I will be covering that as well. Let's start by going through the website which popularized the whole dropshipping business model, which is Shopify.

Shopify

So for people who don't know what Shopify is, Shopify is an e-commerce company founded in Canada. What Shopify provides is an e-commerce platform or an online store for its users. It was originally founded by Scott Lake, Daniel Weinard, and the current CEO, Tobias Lutke. Essentially what Shopify provides you with is a secure online store where you can sell products to consumers online. Most people use this website for online dropshipping rather than warehouse dropshipping since Shopify does not provide users with a warehouse. Starting your very own dropshipping business using Shopify as your platform is very easy and cost effective compared to other platforms.

To start making money with dropshipping using Shopify as your platform, all you will need is a supplier which can ship out the products anywhere in the world for cheap. That's it for the requirements; now I want to get specific with the start-up cost of getting started with Shopify as it is not free, but it is really cost efficient compared to other business models out there.

Now first things first, you will need to buy a domain name. You really need to make sure that your website looks trustworthy, and for that to happen you will need a domain name. Buying a domain name is inexpensive; it will only cost you around $10 to $25 USD per year, depending on the domain name. Now once you get that sorted, you will now have to sign up on Shopify. Since Shopify offers a free 14-day trial, I would recommend you make sure that the store name or brand you decide upon is not taken before you buy a domain name for your website or store. Once you have decided your store name, etc. , it will now be time to buy a package from Shopify which will allow you to start selling your products. Shopify offers three packages, which include

Basic Shopify package ($29.99 USD a month)

Shopify package ($79.99 USD a month)

Advanced Shopify package ($299.99 USD a month)

Also note, if you want to save money you can buy these packages upfront on a yearly basis. But that's totally up to you.

Now you might be wondering which one to get started with. Let me explain each of them to you. If you're just starting your dropshipping business I would like to say right off the bat that you don't need the advanced Shopify package. Once you have your business rolling and if you want to expand, you can do your research on it and upgrade, but for starters, just pick between the basic Shopify package or the Shopify package. If your funds are low, and you want to start making money online then you can totally start off with the basic package, but if you have some extra cash to spare then I would recommend upgrading to the Shopify package as it has some useful benefits.

The useful benefit this Shopify package provides you with, compared to the basic Shopify package, is the lower amount of online credit card rates compared to the basic Shopify package. Even though it's minuscule, it adds up once you start making over thousands of dollars a month. Another great benefit of using the Shopify package compared to the basic Shopify package is that you can start making your own gift cards. As you know, in order to make sales on this platform you will need to get some traffic first before you can actually make some sales online. So having these small incentives can add up to more sales in the future. Other than that these packages are identical. If you will be using Shopify for online dropshipping purposes, you can go with either package which fits your budget. It is up to you which one you want to get started with.

One more thing you can invest in to really make your store stand out are logos, which you will need for your Shopify store. You can get them done professionally by hiring someone on fiverr.com. The logo will not cost you more than $25 USD to get started. If you're able to, you could create the logo yourself, so you wouldn't need to hire someone to make it. Canvas.com is a great tool you could use to make your free logo.

To give a summary of costs so far, to get started with dropshipping using Shopify:

Shopify package $29.99 or $79.99 USD

Domain name $ 10 to $20 USD

Logo around $25 if using someone, otherwise free if created by yourself.

So to get started with Shopify it will cost you $35/45 + $29.99 USD every month

after that, if you go for the cheapest option, or $35/45 + $79.99 every month after that for the next option. Regardless, the costs are not astronomical.

Now, let's talk about the work you will have to put in for your Shopify business to flourish. You will have to make sure your website looks presentable. Shopify provides you with some great themes which can be used to build up your website, no problem. But it does require some work to be put in. Other things you will have to take care of are customer inquiries and complaints. Since it is your brand and company, you will have to deal with everything from complaints to fulfilling an order. So make sure you have an email created for your store inquiries. Also, like I said before, you will have to put emphasis on getting traffic, since no one will know about your store except your family and friends. Other than that, you should be fine.

How you get paid on Shopify is simple as well; all you have to do is make a PayPal account, since some people might choose to complete their transaction using PayPal. Also, Shopify will make you put in your banking information, for the others who use a credit card to make a purchase at your store. Shopify will directly deposit into your account.

The final thing I would like to discuss is how much you can realistically make using Shopify and the online dropshipping method. Since it is your brand and your company, you can make as much as you want. You can become a millionaire or a billionaire with this method, as long as you build a following for your business, which again will be talked about in the later chapters. Overall, the sky is the limit! Work hard and be patient, and you will get what you desire.

Amazon FBA

Unless you have been living under a rock, you know that Amazon is one of the biggest e-commerce companies in the world, with its founder and owner's net worth being a whopping $150 billion dollars, making him the richest man in the world. Jeff Bezos founded his company in the early 90s; his goal was to sell books online. Now Amazon sells everything you can think of. Amazon is the biggest e-commerce company in the world and its website has one of the highest amounts of online traffic in the world. Needless to say, working with Amazon could make you money.

Now you might be wondering, what does the FBA stand for? It stands for Fulfillment By Amazon.

What you have to do in order to a part of this program is simple. First find a product which you can get for cheap, secondly, buy it in bulk, and finally, the third is to ship it to Amazon's warehouse, where it can be shipped off to the customer. It's that simple. Now, the startup cost with this business model is a little bit higher, so let's break it down:

Buying products in bulk for cheap: $1000 - $3000 USD

If you sell more than 40 items a month you will have to pay $39.99

So, on the lower end, you can get started for $1000 USD to $3000 USD plus $39.99 a month if you sell more than 40 products. Plus there is a charge for each product they ship out, but don't worry, it will only be charged once someone orders a product.

Even though there is a bigger upfront investment in this type of dropshipping, it still has some benefits. For example, since your products will be listed on Amazon, you will already be getting free traffic, which would equal higher chances of a sale. Unlike Shopify, Amazon takes care of the back end, like customer refunds, questions, etc. All you do is get the product, ship it to Amazon's warehouse and you will start earning money.

Now let's talk about the work you will have to do in order to get this business started from the ground up. The first thing is finding a cheap supplier. For you to actually make some profits you will have to find products at a low cost. Second, buy it in bulk, and third, ship it to Amazon's warehouse. When business takes off all you will have to worry about is restocking your products by shipping them to Amazon so you can make more money; that's all the work you will have to do. Like I said, all the back end stuff Amazon will take care of, such as shipping, customer service, etc.

So let's talk about how you will get paid on Amazon FBA. It's simple, similar to Shopify. You will first have to make a seller's account on Amazon, and once that is done you will add your banking information to the account. Amazon will pay you the profits you make right into your bank account and you don't have to worry about anything else, besides filing your taxes.

The final thing I would like to talk about is income, how much can you make on Amazon FBA. Since AmazonFBA is not a personal brand which you can grow the income will be limited. I know the top earners can make over two million a year using Amazon FBA, which for some can be amazing to see this kind of cash. But for others who really want to build their brand, Amazon FBA would not be the answer. Now the benefit with this business model is that if you do everything right, you can make money faster and you could scale up higher, but there is a tap on the amount of money you can make here.

eBay

eBay is one the most successful e-commerce websites, founded in 1995 by Pierre Omidyar. It has quickly become a household name around the world. What started as a bidding website online has now become one of the most popular places to sell your items, and it also can be used with great success for drop-shippers all around the world.

Now, starting up with eBay as a dropshipper would probably be the cheapest way to go about it. To get started, all you will need is a supplier who can provide you with cheap products, and a PayPal account to accept payments. There are literally no upfront costs to get started, and you can use the images suppliers have on their pages and upload them to your eBay account. The way eBay makes money is through transactions; once someone purchases a product from you, eBay will take a cut out of that purchase, plain and simple. So to get started with eBay you will need $0 and a cheap connection for your products.

I know, eBay sounds like the best option out of the three right now, but there are some major flaws. The first one is you can't build a brand like you can on Shopify. You see, what appeals to most people is trying out a new brand and seeing what they like. With eBay, it's like buying something for really cheap and on sale, so it will be hard to mark up your products at a higher price like you can on Amazon and Shopify, which will equal fewer profits. Another major problem I see with this method is that it is competing with Amazon, which already has a bigger following and is more trusted by people. So with that in mind, getting organic traffic like you would on Amazon would be hard. So I would recommend spending some money on ads if you want to get sales on eBay. Since the competition on eBay is so high, it will make it really hard for your product to organically sell.

With all that being said, let's talk about how you will be paid on eBay. You will be paid through PayPal, so make sure you have your PayPal account set up. But don't forget eBay will take some money out of the transaction online, plus so will PayPal. So keep that in mind as you move forward.

For everyone who wants to get started with eBay, don't worry, as there is some money to be made. eBay dropshippers can make $1,000 to $3,000 USD as a side income every month, which isn't bad at all, but you can't expect to become a millionaire through eBay. So if you are looking to make a side income, then eBay can definitely fulfill that for you for with no start-up cost.

Now, it's your choice to pick out which website and dropshipping method you want to continue with in starting your own dropshipping business. I know all three of these websites have some amazing benefits but they also come with some issues. For you to find out which type of dropshipping business you want to start with is simple. First ask yourself how much money can you invest, second, ask yourself how much money do you want to make, and then third, how much of this income do you want it to be passive, meaning you don't do a lot of work and you make profits. Now if you have money to invest and want to see returns quickly and have it be passive, then Amazon FBA would be the right fit for you. If your goal is to start your own company and build your own brand, while making amazing amounts of money, then Shopify would be the answer for you. Finally, if you want to make money but you don't have money to invest, then I would highly recommend eBay so you can start earning some side income quickly.

With that being said, I hope this chapter really opened your mind to the different ideas of dropshipping and how much you can make. Like I said, it is up to you to decide on picking the right business model for your needs. It's time for you to evaluate your situation and come up with a business plan that works for you. All three websites can make you money, some more than the others, but again there is a price to pay for each of the websites, so choose wisely.

If you're enjoying this book, I would appreciate it if you went to the place of purchase and left a short positive review. Thank you

Chapter 3: Most profitable niche

So, hopefully, by now, you have decided on which type of dropshipping method and which website you will be moving forward with. Regardless of whichever method you choose, you will need to make sure that your products sell, for you to actually make money. So how will you actually sell products? Well, simply by finding a niche which already has customers and not enough products for all. Here's the cold truth, you will not sell anything or make any money if what you're selling does not have a demand for it. This is why choosing the right niche is imperative for your success in the dropshipping business.

Now, most of you might be wondering what a niche is. Well, to explain it in the most simple manner, a niche is something relating to or being a part of a certain product or service, etc. So, for example, selling something like a dog bracelet to dog lovers, that would be considered a niche. So, as you can see, having a niche to sell in is imperative for your success in this dropshipping business. So in this chapter, what I really want to talk about is how can you find a profitable niche where you can make some amazing profits, without wasting money on buying your products in bulk and letting it sit in the warehouse or paying monthly fees and spending money on advertisements without seeing any profits.

So from my experience with Amazon, Shopify and eBay, when you first initially start you won't be able to make a lot of money in niches which are saturated or have a lot of products to sell. These companies or people will have a lot of money invested in advertisements, and our goal is to get started with minimal money and slowly scale up. The ideal situation for you to make money is to be a big fish in a small pond rather than a small fish in a big pond. Your job is to find a profitable niche which hasn't been tapped into, but you know has potential to sell and make you money.

So to find out a niche which will actually sell and make you money, I have created two ways, or rather I should say two techniques, to find a niche and make money online. So let me first show the websites I use to find a niche which will actually help you make money. The first website I use is Amazon; it is one of the biggest e-commerce websites. So anything that sells well on Amazon will sell anywhere. The second one is Facebook groups and Instagram pages. To find out what you could sell online these pages will help you tremendously. Now let us go into the depths of each way to find a profitable niche. We will begin with Amazon.

Amazon

As we know by now, Amazon is the biggest online store right now. So whatever sells on Amazon sells anywhere, so if your goal is to find a niche which will make you money and is profitable, then you need to review Amazons products.

If you have been to Amazon's website to purchase a product, or anything for that matter, below you will see the best sellers rank under the product description. What that best seller ranks symbolizes is how much of the product is being bought. This is very important for you to note. If the product is not selling on Amazon, which is the biggest e-commerce store in the world, it will not sell anywhere. Now here is what you are going to do in order to find a product that sells.

The very first thing you are going to do is get on your computer and go to Amazon's website. Now what I want you to do is go on to the best sellers page on Amazon. This page will give you a rough idea on what sells and what doesn't, and also will show you the niche products which are selling already. Anything in the Amazon's best sellers page will most likely sell, that is if you can offer it at a cheaper price. Regardless of which platform you will be using for your dropshipping business, if Amazon has the same product for sale that you do, it will have it for the same price or cheaper than you will. This is the case most of the time, but if you can sell it cheaper than your competitors, meaning Amazon, then you have a winning product! Congrats.

Now if that's not the case, it is time to find an untapped niche. So go to the best sellers page on Amazon and look at the top 100 on that list carefully. If you see similar products from the same niche, then this niche is profitable. But it could be hard to penetrate into that specific market or niche. This is where we find a micro-niche. So for example, if the niche is iPhone accessories and there are multiple iPhone accessories on the best sellers list, what we will do is search up iPhone accessories on the Amazon search bar. Then we will go through the top six products and check to see their best sellers list. If the best sellers list showcases a number below 50,000 for all six items, then this niche is profitable.

Hypothetically, you can sell in this niche and make some great profits. But if the competition is high, then there are fewer chances of you actually making profits, so if you want to make sure the completion is low, look at the search engine number. If the search engine number has a number lower than 5,000 items, then the niche is small, and if the top six products have a ranking of lower than 50,000 on the best sellers ranking, then you have a winning product and a niche to get into. So, if you search up iPhone accessories and it has 20,000 items for sale, it would be harder for you tap into, but on the other hand, if you search up iPhone phone cases and it has fewer than 5,000 items for sale and the top six items best seller rank is lower than 50,000, we have a winner at hand. So this is how you use Amazon to find a profitable niche.

Facebook groups and Instagram pages

This is another place where you can find niches to sell in. A lot of Facebook pages and Instagram pages are made to share videos and content online for people to look at, simply because they are a big fan of it. They have a special connection to this niche for some reason; it could be personal, who knows. But you can use this fan page or groups to offer them something they can't refuse.

Think about it, if you were a big fan of dogs and you loved dogs. Wouldn't you want to buy a $25 t-shirt which says "I Love Dogs"? Of course you would, because you are a super-fan. Now the best part about this method is that the people you will advertise your product to will most likely buy it, and there are a lot of pages online where there is a big following but no products to sell. So in order to find these pages, all you will have to do is search and think outside the box, as there are some pages waiting to be sold "I Love something" t-shirts. So look around and search, and once you find your niche, you will making some serious profits.

With all that being said, let me share with you some niches which have made me money in the past:

    Dog lovers
    Cat lovers
    Lion lovers
    Car lovers
    Electronic accessories

These niches are still quite profitable, so do your research, and if you like them, you can sell on these specific niches.

To finish off this chapter, I would just like to remind you how important finding the right niche is. A niche will either make your business or break it, so if you don't do your research before you decide to sell your products online, then you will regret it. Make sure you use the techniques I taught to find the right niches to sell on, and also feel free to use the niches I have personally made money on, as they could make you some money as well. Now, go online and start researching and find the niche you will be selling on.

CHAPTER 4: FINDING SUPPLIERS/WHOLESALERS FOR YOUR BUSINESS

Finding the right supplier or the right wholesalers for your dropshipping business is imperative, meaning that you can't "cheap out" or not care about this aspect. As you can imagine, your business will revolve around your supplier quite heavily. Truth be told, if you don't have any products that you can sell, then it would honestly be impossible for you to make any money, which would therefore be equal to no profits. On the other hand, if you decide to "cheap out" and sell low-quality products, chances are, people will return the products. Even though we discussed the importance of finding a proper niche, to the importance of advertising the product the right way, etc., it can't be overridden by an unreliable or a cheap low-quality product.

Finding the right supplier for your dropshipping business purposes is imperative, for both quality purposes and shipping purposes. Now if you are going to be using Amazon FBA or a similar type of dropshipping method, then shipping times do matter in order for you to stock up your products, but it isn't the biggest deal for that dropshipping model compared to dropshipping methods using Shopify. Now with all that being said, quality is the biggest factor you have to worry about when selling your products. So now we will go through the top websites, from where you can find great suppliers for your business. We will also talk about how to build a great relationship with them, and finally, for everyone dropshipping using the method of online dropshipping, I will reveal a secret to getting the fastest shipping anywhere in the world, so your customers stay happy and fewer refunds are being made.

We will break this chapter into two phases. First, we will talk about how to find suppliers for people using online dropshipping. We will go through everything from finding the product, building a relationship with the seller, getting it shipped fast and of course making sure the product is of a high quality. Then we will talk about finding a supplier or a wholesaler for the warehouse dropshipping method. So with that being said, we begin with online dropshipping.

Online Dropshipping

So, finding a supplier for people using online dropshipping as their business model could be challenging. Since most of the time you will be going by assumptions, what our job with this process is, is to take out as much of the guesswork as we can and find the winning supplier which we are looking for. Now, there are a lot of websites online where you can find products for cheap. But from my experience, AliExpress has one of the best quality product and shipping times. If you have been doing some research online you might have heard things like, "AliExpress is dead," or things of that nature. But I am here to tell you that AliExpress still works amazingly and will help you make some serious profits online. There are some tips and techniques you need to know before you fully start using AliExpress as your sole supplier.

Now, if you don't know what AliExpress is, then let me clarify it for you. Think of AliExpress as the Amazon of China. There are a lot of people selling products online on this website, mostly from China, and as we know most of the products are manufactured in China, meaning the mark up on the products would be a lot less. This means you can easily sell it online for a higher price in the North American market, and to make things even better, the products on AliExpress are mostly similar types of products which are sold or are popular in the North American market. The point I am trying to make is this: people selling on AliExpress are selling to people specifically who want to start their own dropshipping business.

There are some guidelines you need to follow before you start to use AliExpress to dropship products from, as there are some flaws. The things we need to look into before we start selling products using AliExpress are these:

Supplier review

Product photo's and description

E-packet

How many orders sold

Now, if all these points check out, then your supplier is good. So let's begin with the supplier review. To find out if the supplier is good, the first thing you will need to do is check the reviews. Make sure the reviews on their store are at least 95% positive. If that's not the case, then either the product quality isn't good or the product is something else when it gets delivered. Other things to worry about are photos and the description. If the product has great photos and a compelling description, then most of the time it shows that the seller actually cares about what he or she is doing and will do whatever it takes to keep their customers happy.

Another thing to take care of is shipping. If the seller offers a shipping method known as e-packet, then the shipping times will be a lot faster than other suppliers. Normally e-packet delivers the product in 2-3 weeks, which is the fastest shipping time you will get on AliExpress, so make sure your supplier provides you with e-packet. Also, to make sure this supplier is reliable, check out how many orders he/she has had; if it is higher than 500 orders, then they are in the clear. If all the points I just described to you check out, then the supplier is a good supplier and you can truly start to grow your business with him or her, and if the supplier doesn't check out on all these points, then find a new one.

One more tip I would share with you, AliExpress tends to take some time when processing a payment. It could take up to three days. It is done simply for their security. If you want to expedite the process of processing the payment for your order to be shipped even faster, then I would recommend using AliPocket. AliPocket is similar to a gift card. It is like a safe credit card for AliExpress, so if you buy AliPocket in bulk and use it to buy the product which you will be shipping out to your client, then there would be no time wasted for processing a payment, and the order will be shipped right away.

Now, AliExpress is great for selling new, trending stuff. But if your goal is to sell fan t-shirts and things of that nature, then it might not be the right choice for you. AliExpress has a lot of things to sell online, but the products it sells are not specific to niches, and people, this is where print on demand t-shirts come in.

What is print on demand, you might ask. Well, print on demand is a service where you come up with a logo, pick out a plain t-shirt, sweater or whatever they have, then what will happen is that the company will use your logo, put it on a t-shirt, etc., and directly ship it out to the customer or the buyer. That is what print on demand is. Now there are a lot of websites to choose from. But the one I highly recommend is Pillow Profits. It is amazing; not only do they have your good old t-shirts, but they also offer things like pillowcases, shower curtains, bed sheets, etc., which can be sent to a customer with your logo on any of those things.

Now print on demand is ideal for those super niche fan pages we talked about before. Since those fan pages are unique and hard to find, you need to be really unique with your products, just like the page you are promoting it to. So, if your store is based on super-niche products, then it would be hard to find products on AliExpress, and this is where print on demand comes in.

What print on demand will offer you is this: cheap supplies with whatever you want on it and fast shipping. Most of the print on demand websites have a really fast delivery since most of them are based in the United States, so you don't need to worry about shipping or any of that. Just make sure to pick out a print on demand website you like and come up with a logo.

Let us talk about building relationships with your suppliers. It is imperative that you build a great relationship with your supplier. Not only will it help you make more profits, but it will also help you get faster shipping times. What I am about to tell you applies more to AliExpress rather than print on demand websites. Regardless of which website it is, you need a great relationship with your supplier, so in order to build great relationships with your suppliers here are the ways you can do so.

Give them business

Be accepting

Leave them great reviews

So, giving them business is quite self-explanatory. If you want to build a great relationship you have to give them business. You can't expect to be their "special customer" if you don't buy anything from them. So make sure you first buy at least 20-25 items before you think about asking them for a discount on your

products. Another thing to be mindful about is making sure you don't get angry at them for a shipment which is a couple of days late, or things of that nature. You have to remember they are trying their best to keep you happy, just like you are trying to keep your customers happy. So make sure you are being accepting and not making a big deal about small things like these. The final thing is to leave a positive review because, let us face it, everyone cares about positive reviews. If you follow all these steps, you will start to build a great relationship with your supplier and you can slowly start to ask for things like discounts on your orders, which would mean a higher profit margin for you. So make sure you start to build a great relationship with them.

With all that said, that is all for finding a supplier for people using online dropshipping. Let's talk about finding suppliers for people using Amazon FBA or warehouse dropshipping. It is a little bit different but shares some of the same principles.

Warehouse dropshipping

To find suppliers or products for this type of dropshipping is a little bit easier compared to online dropshipping. Since you can inspect all the product before you start selling, it makes it one step easier compared to the others. So, in short, there are three ways you can go about finding a supplier. The first one is using sites like AliExpress, the second one is to find a warehouse where they are selling the products for cheap, and finally buy products on special sales and re-sell them.

Now, you already know how to find the right supplier on AliExpress, but let's talk about how you can use AliExpress for warehouse dropshipping. So right off the bat, once you find a product that you would like to sell I would highly recommend you buy one of the products and really check its quality. Once you have checked it out and made sure that the quality is of a high caliber, then you should contact the supplier and work out a deal. You see, since you will be buying the product in bulk there would be more chance of you actually getting it for a further discounted price, so make sure you ask for it so you can make even more profit. Finally, once that is all done, ship it to the warehouse and start selling.

That was using AliExpress. Now, let's talk about using warehouse or special sales to find your supplies. People don't realize that there are a lot of warehouses like Costco where you can buy stuff for cheap and sell it on Amazon. So the way this process works is simple. Go to a warehouse like Costco, find a product in bulk for really cheap, and then transport it to Amazon's warehouse and start selling. Trust me, I have found so many cheap products at Costco for sale which have made me some great profits! Make sure you find these products and start selling them on Amazon.

Finally, one of the ways I have made tremendous amounts of money on Amazon FBA is by waiting for sales like Black Friday, and things of that nature. I would buy products on sale for 50% to even 70% off, and after the sale is done I would sell it on Amazon at its original price. Although this method is not as frequently occurring as the other two, it will yield you a lot of profits, so make sure you wait for these sales to make some real cash.

Finally, one secret method I have used before is finding listings on Craigslist and Facebook marketplaces for products and supplies. Most of the time, you will find brand new stuff for sale near you, and the seller would be selling it off for next to nothing. So this would be your time to shine. Find something in bulk for really cheap on these websites, work out a deal, and sell it off on Amazon for a great profit. Now if you find something for cheap but the quantity is low, then I would recommend using eBay to sell it on. I remember finding a brand new iPhone for super cheap, so just like anyone else would do, I bought it and sold it off on eBay for a great profit. So whatever you can find on these websites for cheap, make sure to act on them as soon as possible before they are gone.

So to conclude this chapter, I would just like to remind you how important it is to have the right supplier. A great supplier can either make your business or break it. Making sure you have the right supplier is imperative, as it will only help you have a longer sustained business. So please, make sure you read this chapter very carefully and practice all the tricks and techniques taught in this chapter in order for you to find the right supplier. Don't settle for a product or supplier which "gets the job done." If you want your business to be the best it can be, then find a product or supplier which would be the best you can find in terms of service quality, and of course the price. But also don't forget to keep your suppliers happy; like I said, if you want better deals on your products you need to make sure your relationship with your supplier is great.

That's all for this chapter; see you on the next one.

CHAPTER 5: FINDING A HIGHLY PROFITABLE PRODUCT

Does anyone remember the product, the fidget spinner? It came out a couple of years ago and it was really famous. As you can imagine, it made a lot of money, from the people who created it to anyone who sold it. Whoever sold the product when it was at its peak made a whole lot of money. People were buying that product like it was water; it truly became a necessity. It was wild!

You see, the fidget spinner is an example of a highly profitable product, and from the title, you might have guessed it, yes, we are going to be talking about highly profitable products and how to find them. Now here's the good news: finding a profitable product is easy, but to sell it at the right place and the right time is when it gets a tad bit tricky.

Before we get started with this chapter I want to tell you what a product is and the different types of products. So, a product is something you trade or give someone for money.... mostly money. Now there are two types of products. The first one is a commodity product, and the second one would be considered a niche product. A commodity product would be something every human needs for survival. A couple of examples would be bread, water, car, etc. These products are needed by most people so they can survive or sustain a certain lifestyle, which means they will do whatever it takes to get these products to survive.

Now the other product is a niche based product. A niche product would be something people don't buy out of necessity; rather they buy it because they like it. So an example of these products would be dog bracelets, GI Joes, etc. So by no means would you need these products for survival, but there is definitely a need for them.

Ideally, we would all like to sell in the commodity niche as there is a constant demand for it. But to sell things of the commodity type would be a bit challenging, since the people who are at the top of the food chain have spent so much money on the commodity products that in order for you to sell and actually make good money, you would have to spend a lot of money on advertisement. Now, to get into a niche product can work and can make you money. But even though there is less competition, it can be hard to get into.

Remember the fidget spinner I was talking about earlier? What kind of product do you think it is? Commodity or a niche product? If your answer was niche, then you are completely wrong. A fidget spinner was a combination of both commodity AND a niche product. The fidget spinner was a product which was made for people who needed something to fidget with, and through advertising and popularity became a commodity. Do you see where I"m going with this? If you want to find a winning product, find one which is both a commodity product and a niche based product.

So how do you actually go about finding a commodity product and a niche product? Let's discuss. As we know, clothing is worn by everyone and everyone will buy clothes, some people more often than others. If someone is selling a puppy, would you honestly buy it? Would it be a commodity? No, you don't need to have a puppy to survive. It is more of an interest or a niche specific thing to get a puppy. Now for a puppy fan who isn't ready to take on a responsibility of a puppy, what would he or she buy? A puppy or a really cool puppy t-shirt? Obviously a puppy t-shirt. When you combine a commodity product with a niche based product, you really start to create something beautiful. So make sure you create or find something like that.

Now, that is one example of finding or creating a winning product. The next place you can actually find great products to start selling online would be using a website called Thieve.co. This website is impressive; not only does it show the most trending product right now on the market but it also hooks you up with the seller. You know what the best part about this website is? It's that it shows the most trending products based on niche, so if you want to find your winning product to sell online, then I would definitely check out Thieve.co.

Also, if you remember, I spoke about Amazon, to find a niche to sell into. Well, Amazon can be used for finding a winning product as well! If you go into the best sellers rank and look up the top 100 best seller products, then chances are, you will find a product that sells for you. Guys, don't forget, Amazon is the biggest e-commerce store, so if people are actually buying from Amazon, that means it sells. Another website you can use it AliExpress. If you want to find a winning product, then go on AliExpress and look at the best sellers. Since most of the dropshippers use AliExpress as their supplier for their dropshipping business, if the product sells on AliExpress, it most likely will sell for you, because drop-shippers are selling it to their customers. Another great technique is to check out other Shopify websites and to check out what they are selling. Sometimes checking out your competitors' products can help you find that winning product you have been looking for. One of the ways I find out about other Shopify websites is by going to Shopifyexchange.com. What they do is sell Shopify websites which are already making money, so if I were you, I would go on their website and check out their winning products and try and sell them in your store. And most of the time, it works.

The final tool I would recommend is using a software called Dropship Spy. It is a software which shows you the newest and the latest products online, and although there a small amount to be paid for it, it is totally worth it. If you are really serious about starting your dropshipping business, I would recommend you get this software. Just be aware that this system is more for online dropshippers rather than warehouse dropshippers, so keep that in mind.

After you have done everything to find your winning product, what you need to know is how to advertise it. You will not find out how good the product is or how "revolutionary" the product is unless you advertise it and try to sell it. Don't worry, in the next chapter we will talk about how to advertise your product the right way using Facebook and other various tools. If the product doesn't sell after following all the steps above, then find out what you did wrong in finding the right product, then rinse and repeat. Find a new product to sell and make sure you don't make any mistakes this time, finding a new product. You will not find a winning product in your first try, unless you are very fortunate. The point is that it may take time and research to find the right product to sell for your drop shipping, so be patient and stay true to the process, and you will eventually find your winning product.

So that is all the things I wanted to talk about in this chapter. Make sure you follow everything I have said in this chapter if you want to find a winning product. If you have a feeling that this new product you stumbled upon might be the next fidget spinner, then do your research, make sure that you are correct and take the risk. Although it is important to be safe and smart about investing in a new product, sometimes it is also important that you take some risks. Sometimes those risky products yield the best results, which end up making you money. Finally, for people out there trying to create a commodity and niche product in one, make sure whatever you're selling really hits the buyer emotionally. People will buy anything if it attracts them emotionally, so make sure the product isn't more of a commodity product to a niche or vice versa. That is all for this chapter; see you in the next one.

If you're enjoying this book, I would appreciate it if you went to the place of purchase and left a short positive review. Thank you

Chapter 6: How to market your business

By now, this book has commented on all major aspects of dropshipping, from the different types of dropshipping businesses, how to start your own dropshipping business, and how to pick out the most profitable niche and products. You see, everything is important for your business to flourish, but if you can't get people to come onto your page/website or drive traffic to it, then nothing in this book will help you get sales. It's simple; if no one is there to see your product or what you're selling, then no one is going buy your product. It's just going to sit there and do nothing. So for you to make sales, you need to drive some traffic to your store or page, and that is what we will be talking about in this chapter: how to drive traffic to your store or page.

Learning how to drive traffic can be a challenging task. There is no right or wrong answer in this method. For some people, using websites like Facebook and Instagram could work amazingly and that is all they do to drive traffic, whereas for others, using free traffic techniques could be working beautifully, making them some serious sales. So, it is more trial and error than getting it right in the first place.

When I started my dropshipping business, I tried everything, from Facebook ads to free traffic techniques like creating blogs, and sending out emails. But all my dropshipping businesses work differently, and sometimes one business would work great on getting Facebook traffic and only that, while others might work great on blog traffic or emails, so it really just depends. So to find out what works and what doesn't, you need to try it out and see for yourself. There is no way to tell if a specific ad will generate you millions of dollars or not.

We will talk about the three biggest ways to drive traffic to your product page or website, which are Facebook ads, Instagram shout outs and finally, free traffic utilizing blogs, emails, etc. Try all of them to see which works out best for you. You may find more success with one rather than the other. In my opinion, the hardest one is Facebook. So let's tackle that first.

Facebook

Facebook has over 2 billion users. So naturally, there will be many people on Facebook who may be interested in buying your products. Facebook advertisements have been used by almost every dropshipper you can find to drive traffic. This method is probably the cheapest and the most effective method you can use to drive traffic to your product page or store. Now, there are some steps you need to go through before you start advertising your product the right way by utilizing Facebook, which we will be going through in this chapter.

First things first. When you create your Facebook ads account, you will need to make sure you add your website pixel on it. This is important for people using the online dropshipping method. Here is the thing; if you don't add your store pixel onto your Facebook ads account, it will not be able to collect data for your website and products. The pixel will collect things like what kind of people are checking out your product page and what kind of people are actually purchasing your product, which would equal a better ad campaign in the future, as you would be able to target specific people to your product page or website. Now, after you have created your Facebook ads account and added your pixel to your Facebook ads account, we can now start to advertise your products. Here is what we need to take care of before we start advertising on Facebook:

Finding products like yours

Finding big companies' Facebook ads

Targeting to a certain age group and country

Amazing product photos

Amazing captions

Split testing

I know, there are a lot of things to worry about. But believe it or not, these are just the basics we need to take care of, as there a lot of other advertising methods which can be used. But for now, worry about the basics.

So let's start off with the first step. Finding a similar product to yours on Google is important to look for, as most of the time it will show you the top sellers of your niche. When you start your Facebook ad campaign, it will ask you for ad pages or companies related to your niche. Our job is quite simple, yet important. The first thing we will do is go online and search up our product. For example, if I am selling a car, I will look up "cars for sale," then I would click on all the websites which sell our products. So in this hypothetical scenario, I would be clicking through Honda, Toyota, etc. So, after you do that, I want you to write down all the websites which are related to the niche or product that you are going to be selling.

After you have all the top websites, I want you to log into Facebook. Then after that is done, I want you to search up the websites' Facebook pages. Once you have done that, check to see if their Facebook likes are over 500,000, and if so, you have found a winner. You see, what Facebook does with that information on your campaign is this; it will promote your product to the specific people on that page. So let's get back to my hypothetical scenario. If I am selling a car and I add Honda to my targeted Facebook advertisement, it will then specifically target people who are interested in Honda. So find: one, a product, two, a Facebook page which has over 500k followers, and three, the product to the people interested in that page.

Now that you have the keywords and the specific people you will be advertising your products to, it is now time to create an eye-catching advertisement. Since most of you haven't created a Facebook advertisement, I assume, so in order for you to make sure your advertisement converts into sales you will need to make sure your ads look good. Now there are many tips and techniques out there spelled out by "supposed" dropshipping gurus, but some of you might have heard the phrase "If it ain't broke, don't fix it," meaning that if there are big companies advertising their products successfully, then there is no need to come up with your own different unique way of doing it, as that trial and error could hurt your wallet.

If you did your research and tried to find big websites or companies specific to your niche, then there is a high chance that you might have seen their Facebook ads pop up. The next time you see them, I really want you to examine their advertising and see what kind of video or images they are using. This will help you build your own advertisement, so make sure you review the ads and copy what they are doing. Trust me, it will work a lot better than you creating your own special ones.

Let's talk about finding age groups and country for your advertisements. If you know what your product provides to consumers, you would know what kind of people would be interested in purchasing your products. Before you start your first campaign on Facebook, it will ask you to put an age range on your advertisement. So if you are going to be selling a car like I am, then I would probably set the age range around 25 to 65 as most of the people 18 years old won't be buying one by themselves and anyone over 65 won't either. So our goal is to target people who are most likely to buy your product, so this takes some research and there some guesswork involved. But if you really specify the age, you will save a good amount of money and get more sales.

Whereas for picking out the country or region to advertise it to, I would recommend you advertise it to the US only if your budget is small. Most of your buyers will be coming from the United States, so no need to worry about advertising it to any other people. Now, if you have some spare change left over, then you can extend your audience to Canada, which could get you more views and more sales.

After you have done all of this research it's now time to create your advertising image and caption. People don't realize how important it is for you to have the right image and caption for your post. This will either make your post or break it. So picking out the right photo and caption is imperative for your advertisement to be a success. Now how do you pick out the right image for your advertisement? Simple; if you did your research correctly looking up big companies' websites, then you will know the specific type of photo or caption to use, so mimic their advertisement.

Now, after you have decided upon the photos and caption you will be going with, it is now time to add the photo to your campaign. Two things to remember: make sure the photo is high-definition. If it is not high-definition, then it won't stand out from the crowd and it will also look unprofessional. Also make sure the photo is compatible on a smartphone advertisement. To check out what it would look like on a smartphone, simply click on the smartphone advertisement option. It will show you what it looks like.

Now let's talk about the caption. For you to get people clicking on the caption you need to make sure that it is eye-catching. To deliver a great caption you need to make sure you offer your clients some incentives, such as "GET THIS NOW. 50% OFF" or "ONLY 50 LEFT IN STOCK". In the same manner that big firms advertise, you will need to make sure you create urgency by adding an incentive.

Finally, when everything is good to go and ready to be launched, you can utilize a tool called split testing. What you have to do is create two similar advertising campaigns with slight changes. For example, one ad could have an age group of 18-50 and the other 25-65. After the ad has been running for some time, it will show you which one works better compared to the other. This will help you optimize your ad campaigns in the future. This is optional but highly recommended.

That is all for Facebook advertising. Let's now talk about Instagram Influencer advertising.

Instagram

Instagram is a great place to advertise your products. They have an enormous number of users and most of the time they are more engaged, as compared to Facebook. So if you are thinking about dismissing the idea of advertising on Instagram, think again, as you would be leaving a lot on the table. Note that advertising from Facebook does go on onto Instagram, but it isn't as potent as it should be. So when advertising on Instagram, we use a method called "Instagram Influencer." What it is is quite simple. First, you will find an Instagram page which is related to your topic. Second, you will ask them to promote your product on their Instagram page, and finally, see sales come in. I have used a lot of methods, but this one always works! If you want quick sales on your Instagram account, use this method. Now let's talk about the things you need to worry about before you start advertising on Instagram:

Find the right influencer

Make sure they don't have any bots

Engagement

So, the thing is, for you to make sales and rack up a reasonable amount of cash from your sales, you will need to make sure that your influencer has the right audience. You cannot expect to make sales off of a dog bracelet if the page is about "I hate dogs."

This would not make sense. Make sure the product you are trying to sell is related to the audience who relate to that specific page. So for example, if I want to sell a fishing rod, I would look up, say, fishing areas, or great places to fish, and promote there.

Now, before you go out finding your influencer page, you need to make sure that the page has at least 300k followers. If it doesn't, then you are not going to get the engagement you are looking for.

Next thing to take care of would be making sure the influencer you are thinking about working with has a great engagement rate. If people are not tuning into their page ,they probably won't see your ads as well. There are some tools you can use to find that out, but if someone is not getting at least 5-10% of their followers, meaning if they have 100k followers and they are not getting at least 5-10k likes, then the chances are, the followers are not engaging.

This would also show you if the followers are bots or not, meaning if they have bought followers or if they are real followers.

Now let's talk about how to get a shout from these Instagram pages. Message them directly, saying you want a shout out. Then once you guys work out a deal, ask them for a "story shout out," as those work the best. Ask for a 12-hour story shout out; all the followers will see your advertisement within the 12 hours, so no need to advertise it longer than you should.

With that being said, let's now discuss the third method.

Blogs and emails

This method works great! If someone has already bought from you once, and they liked the product or your services, chances are they will buy from you again. Using tools like creating your own blogs or anything of that nature can work beautifully for you to get sales and or to get some traffic into your store, so there are a lot of ways you can get free traffic. We will only be talking about the two main ones today, which would be creating a blog, and collecting an email list. Now there is a downside to this method. It could take some time to get traffic to your blog and collecting an email list, so don't consider this method if you want fast results.

Using blogs and email lists to promote your products and services have been used for some time now, a lot of successful dropshipping businesses solely use this method to advertising their products and services. So it works, and it works great! Just remember, it won't work right away as it takes time.

Now, with that said, here are three things you need to worry about before you start advertising with this method:

Create a blog

Get traffic on the blog

Collect email subscribers

Email them, not SPAM!

So, the first thing you need to do is to create a blog. You will need to create a blog in order for you to actually start collecting emails. So how you actually collect emails is quite simple, Once you have created a blog, I want you to start publishing about the niche or subject which relates to your store or product. For example, if your online store or your product is regarding fishing, then write a blog about "how to ice fish," etc. Make sure the blog you write is filled with knowledge. People would not want to subscribe to a blog if it is not interesting or providing them with great tricks and tips about the niche.

Now, once you have created a blog and written your first blog, you will now need to start promoting your blog to the right people. This can be done for free; all you have to do is go on Google and search up similar blogs posted in the 24 hour mark time. Go on their blog's comment section and tell every reader to check out your link! It works great and equals free traffic.

After you have started to get some traffic onto your website, it will now be time to collect some emails. In order for you to collect emails, offer them something. So, if your blog and store are related to fitness, offer them a free workout plan if they enter their email! Everyone wants free stuff, so make sure you offer it to them. This should help you collect your email list. I have personally built up around 10,000 email lists using this technique, so make sure you use it.

Once you have a good amount of emails you can now start promoting your products. But there is one thing you should not forget: this is not spam! People do not like to see a sales email every day, so make sure you space it out. Ideally here is how you should go about emailing your potential client. For the first four days, send them an educational email like "How to Fish" or "How to Workout," again, something related to your website, and then on the fourth day, you can try and promote your product. This strategy normally works for me, and I am certain that it would work for you.

Now, with that said, I would like to finish off this chapter. Please remember that not all of your advertising or ad campaigns will work. Some might fail and some might work and make you a lot of profit. Your job is to find out what works for you and what doesn't. So trial and error is the answer, but if you follow everything to a T, then you will see success quicker than you had expected. Also, don't forget to try every method out before you knock it, because some methods take time and they might work great for you later on, so keep trying. Success will eventually come your way.

CONCLUSION

Thank you for sticking it through and reading *Dropshipping: How to generate passive income using e-commerce advanced strategies, Shopify, Amazon FBA and eBay* till the end. I just hope this information was super useful for you to start your very own dropshipping business. The information and knowledge in this book can be useful to a beginner all the way to advanced dropshippers, as the knowledge in this book comes from experience.

The next step for you would be to read all the chapters very carefully, and make sure that whatever is written in the book is absorbed by your brain. From picking out the method you will be using for dropshipping, all the way to finding the right niche to get into reading and finalizing it. Write down notes if you have to, do whatever you can in order to make sure the knowledge in the book doesn't go to waste.

Once you have finally absorbed all the knowledge in this book, I want you to act on it. Act on your goals; if your goal is to start dropshipping to start earning money, then do it! Don't wait. Most people tend to learn about a new topic or business and most of the time they do start, but they give up as soon as they hit their first road bump.

You have to remember that in any business there will be ups and downs so don't expect everything to go smoothly and efficiently. You will fail sometimes. Sometimes you will lose some money. That's the cold hard truth. But if you keep going at your goals, you will eventually get there. Just remember to start and to not give up.

Finally, I would like to remind you this. Every successful person failed at first before he achieved his or her goal. Do you think Jeff Bezos grew his company to where it is today by not facing any adversity? Probably not. Look, I am not trying to scare you before you get into this business. I am just motivating you to not give up as most people do. Just remember that everything takes time and hard work, so keep going at it. If you really want it, it will happen for you. Just work hard and don't give up. Success is on its way!